Amazing Ethiopian Foods

The Best Ethiopian Cookbook

Have Fun Cooking Ethiopian Food

By

Martha Stephenson

License Notes

No part of this Book can be reproduced in any form or by any means including print, electronic, scanning or photocopying unless prior permission is granted by the author.

All ideas, suggestions and guidelines mentioned here are written for informative purposes. While the author has taken every possible step to ensure accuracy, all readers are advised to follow information at their own risk. The author cannot be held responsible for personal and/or commercial damages in case of misinterpreting and misunderstanding any part of this Book

Table of Contents

Introduction..5

Chapter 1. Wonderful Ethiopian Appetizers......................10

Special Ethiopian Cheese Sambusa Turnovers......................11

Delicious Meat Sambusa Turnovers 13

Ethiopian Veggie Sambusa Turnovers..........................15

Party Green Pepper Relish 18

Ethiopian Buticha...19

Ethiopian Dabo Kolo 21

Chapter 2. Delicious Ethiopian Bread Recipes...................23

Injera Bread...24

Delicious Ambasha Bread......................................26

Ethiopian Honey Bread..28

Ethiopian Instant Bread (Kita Firfir)............................30

Ethiopian Steamed Bread (Hibist) 32

Chapter 3. Special Ethiopian Salad Recipes......................34

Delicious Azifa (Green Lentils Salad)...........................35

Special Ethiopian Tomato Salad 37

Delicious Eggplant Salad......................................39

Ethiopian Potato Salad..41

Amazing Ethiopian Green Salad................................43

Ethiopian Beet and Potato Salad...............................45

Chapter 4. Delicious Ethiopian Soups and Stews 47

    Tomato and Lentil Soup (Shorba Addis) 48

    Special Ethiopian Carrot Soup 50

    Delicious Ethiopian Chicken and Butter Soup 52

    Delicious Ethiopian Beetroot Soup 54

    Amazing Ethiopian Chicken Stew 56

    The Best Ethiopian Stew (Alicha) 58

    Wonderful Ethiopian Pumpkin Stew 60

    Tasty Ethiopian Beef Stew 62

    Ethiopian Lentils Stew 65

Chapter 5. Authentic Ethiopian Main Courses 67

    Delicious Ethiopian Steak 68

    Ethiopian Sautéed Fish Dish (Yasa Tibs) 70

    Amazing Ethiopian Chicken 72

    Amazing Ethiopian Spinach and Cottage Cheese 74

    Great Ethiopian Lamb 76

    Ethiopian Beef Steak Tartar 78

Chapter 6. The Most Popular Ethiopian Drinks Recipes 80

    Ethiopian Spiced Tea 81

    Ethiopian Punch 82

    Ethiopian Telba 84

    Tej (Ethiopian Honey Wine) 86

    Delicious Ethiopian Coffee (Kahawa) 87

Conclusion 88

About the Author 89

Author's Afterthoughts 91

Introduction

Ethiopia- A True Culinary Adventure!

Over the last 30 years, Ethiopian cuisine has gained a lot of popularity to its complexity and refinement. More and more people consider it as an amazing combination between different indigenous cuisines: amhara, tagrayan, oromo, gurage and some African tribes.

Ethiopian cuisine is characterized by extremely powerful and distinct tastes like sour, salty, hot, spicy and sweet. These combinations are all based on the usage of amazing local herb, spices and vegetables.

Ethiopian foods are always well balanced and beautifully created.

The Most Popular Ingredients

The main ingredients used in Ethiopian cuisine are cereals, fresh or dried meat, legumes, roots, veggies and fruits.

The main cereals used in Ethiopian dishes are: wheat (sende), corn (boqqolo), teff, barley (gabs) and sorghum (masella).

An important part of Ethiopian dishes is the bread like injera, dabbo or qitta and they are all made from these cereals.

Also, these cereals are used to prepare some meals called "genfo" which are served during festive times like weddings or births.

Genfos are served with a combination of butter and berbere (the most important spice blend used in Ethiopian cuisine)

The main legumes used in Ethiopian cuisine are peas, lentils and beans. These are used to prepare so called "seros" or "kekks".

Beef is considered to be a very special meat. People often sacrifice these animals in order to sell the meat. They rarely eat the meat but when then do, they usually divide it in equal parts, each containing an organ, a bone and a muscle and then they cook it.

Other main ingredients of Ethiopian dishes are potatoes and cabbage. These are used in different stews called "wat" or soups, which are called "maraq".

Also, Ethiopian dishes contain a lot of chili peppers, black, red and white ground pepper, coriander and ginger.

The Most Popular Ethiopian Dishes

As you can see, there are some very popular Ethiopian dishes that everyone enjoys there.

Let's learn more about them.

Injera is their most popular bread. It is made of teff and it is served with almost everything.

Fit- fit is made from fresh bread called "kitcha", "berbere" and "niter kibbeh" and it is usually served for breakfast.

Another very popular Ethiopian dish is called "dulet" and it is also served as a breakfast. It is made of beef oranges and belly, spices and chili peppers and it is served with injera bread.

"Fatira" is a big pancake, toasted, made from wheat flour and it is generally served with honey and eggs. "berbere" and "niter kibbeh".

Another traditional Ethiopian food is called "kitfo" and it contains raw beef meat, marinated in a paprika based spice blend called "mitmita" and "niter kibbeh".

Sorghum is used to make a delicious snack called "kolo". The best "kolo" snack is called "dabo kolo" which is very tasty.

The Most Popular Ethiopian Drinks

Ethiopia is also called "the country of good coffee". They enjoy delicious coffees with "wat, "tibs", "berbere" and "injera".

Another famous Ethiopian drink is called "tej" and it is generally served after official dinner parties.

They also drink a lot of teas and different kinds of punch.

All in all, despite the fact that Ethiopia is considered to be a poor country with important differences between the rich and the poor people, Ethiopian cuisine is simply fabulous and worth trying.

So, don't think too much! Just purchase "Amazing Ethiopian Foods- The Best Ethiopian Cookbook- Have Fun Cooking Ethiopian Food " and start cooking right away!

It's so much fun!

Chapter 1. Wonderful Ethiopian Appetizers

The Ethiopian cuisine is full of incredible and unique dishes. We'll start our wonderful journey with some of the best and most popular Ethiopian appetizers.

Special Ethiopian Cheese Sambusa Turnovers

It's one of the most delicious Ethiopian appetizers you'll ever have!

Preparation time: 5 minutes

Total time: 20 minutes

Yield: 6

Ingredients:

- 6 kiri cheeses
- 3 garlic cloves finely chopped
- 1 small yellow onion finely chopped
- 2 tablespoons feta cheese
- 2 tablespoons milk
- ¼ cup mozzarella finely grated
- 3 tablespoons cilantro finely chopped
- 3 tablespoons carrots finely grated
- 12 Sambusa wrappers
- Vegetable oil for frying
- Flour paste for sealing (flour mixed with water until you obtain a paste)

Method:

1. In a bowl, mix kiri with feta and mozzarella cheese.

2. Add milk and garlic and stir well.

3. Also add carrots, cilantro and onion and stir again.

4. Fill sambusa wrappers with 1 tablespoon cheese mix and seal edges well with flour paste.

5. Heat up a large pan with enough vegetable oil for frying over medium high heat, add a batch of cheese sambusa, fry until they become golden, transfer to paper towels and drain excess fat.

6. Repeat with the rest of the sambusa wraps, arrange on a plate and serve.

Enjoy!

Delicious Meat Sambusa Turnovers

Here's another interesting Sambusa recipe. Try it and enjoy!

Preparation time: 5 minutes

Total time: 25 minutes

Yield: 6

Ingredients:

- 1 pound ground chuck
- 1 yellow onion finely chopped
- 2 garlic cloves finely grated
- 8 ounces sambusa wrappers
- Ground cardamom to the taste
- Salt and black pepper to the taste
- A pinch of cayenne pepper
- Vegetable oil for frying
- Flour paste for sealing

Method:

1. Heat up a pan over medium high heat, add meat, season with salt and pepper to the taste and cook until it becomes brown.

2. Drain excess grease, add garlic, onion, cardamom and cayenne pepper, stir and cook for 4-5 minutes.

3. Take meat off heat and leave aside until it cools down.

4. Fill each sambusa wrappers with 1 tablespoon meat mixture and seal edges with flour paste.

5. Heat up a pan with the vegetable oil over medium high heat, drop sambosas, deep fry them, drain them on paper towels, arrange on a platter and serve them.

Enjoy!

Ethiopian Veggie Sambusa Turnovers

If you are not in the mood for a cheese sambusa or a meat one, then we offer you a vegetarian alternative! It's as good as the others! Or even better!

Preparation time: 10 minutes

Total time: 1 hour

Yield: 12

Ingredients:

- 3 cups water
- 1 cup lentils
- 2 potatoes chopped
- 2 inch finger piece finely chopped
- 1 big carrot chopped
- 7 garlic cloves chopped
- 1 yellow onion finely chopped
- 1 green chili pepper chopped
- 1 red bell pepper chopped
- 2 tablespoons extra virgin olive oil
- 2 teaspoons garam masala
- 2 teaspoons curry powder
- 1 teaspoon paprika
- 1 teaspoon cumin
- 1 teaspoon chili powder
- Salt to the taste

- ½ teaspoon red pepper flakes
- 12 sambusa wrappers
- Cooking spray

Method:

1. Put lentils in a pan, add water to cover, place on stove over medium high heat, bring to a boil, reduce heat to medium and simmer for 25 minutes.

2. Heat up a pan with the olive oil over medium heat, add onions, stir and cook for 5 minutes.

3. Add carrot, potatoes, chili powder, salt, pepper flakes, curry powder, garam masala, paprika and cumin, stir and cook for 5 more minutes.

4. Add bell pepper, green chili, garlic and ginger, stir and cook for 10 minutes.

5. Drain lentils, add them to the veggie mix as well and cook for 10 minutes.

6. Spray a baking sheet with some cooking spray.

7. Fill each sambosa wrapper with the veggie mix, seal edges, arrange them on the baking sheet, spray some cooking oil on them, introduce in the oven at 375 degrees, take them out of the oven, flip and spray them again and bake for another 10 minutes.

8. Leave them to cool down when they're done, arrange on a platter and serve.

Enjoy!

Party Green Pepper Relish

Try this Ethiopian relish for your next party and you'll see that everyone will ask for more!

Preparation time: 10 minutes

Total time: 10 minutes

Yield: 4

Ingredients:

- 1 big green bell pepper roughly chopped
- Salt and black pepper to the taste
- 1 big garlic clove chopped
- 1 jalapeno chili chopped
- Toasted whole wheat bread for serving

Method:

1. Put bell pepper and garlic in your food processor and pulse a few times.

2. Add salt and pepper to the taste and the jalapeno and pulse again until you obtain a paste.

3. Serve with toasted whole wheat bread slices.

Enjoy!

Ethiopian Buticha

This is a traditional Ethiopian spread you can easily serve as an appetizer!

Preparation time: 5 minutes

Total time: 5 minutes

Yield: 4

Ingredients:

- 1 teaspoon red chili flakes
- 1 cup chickpeas already cooked, drained and rinsed
- 2 tablespoons olive oil
- 1 cup water
- Salt and black pepper to the taste
- ½ cup red onion finely chopped
- 1 teaspoon mustard
- Juice from ½ lemon

Method:

1. Put chickpeas in your food processor.

2. Add chili flakes and the oil and pulse a few times.

3. Add water, salt, pepper, mustard, lemon juice and red onion and pulse again well until you obtain a paste.

4. Transfer to a serving bowl and keep in the fridge until you serve it.

Enjoy!

Ethiopian Dabo Kolo

It's both a party appetizer and a tasty midday snack! It's your choice!

Preparation time: 10 minutes

Total time: 15 minutes

Yield: 24 pieces

Ingredients:

- ½ tablespoon sugar
- 1 cup white flour
- A pinch of salt
- ½ teaspoon berbere paste
- ¼ cup water
- 2 tablespoons extra virgin olive oil
- Some melted butter

Method:

1. In a bowl, mix flour with berbere paste, salt and olive oil.

2. Stir very well until your obtain a dough and start adding water gradually.

3. Knead your dough for 5 minutes, take pieces from the dough, place them on a floured working surface, make strips using your palms and cut strips in ½ inches.

4. Put your snacks in a heated pan over medium high heat and with no oil.

5. Leave them to cook until they become golden turning them from time to time.

6. Take them off heat, arrange them on a serving plate and serve.

Enjoy!

Chapter 2. Delicious Ethiopian Bread Recipes

A traditional Ethiopian meal must always contain bread.
Therefore, it's our duty to present to you the most popular
Ethiopian bread recipes.

Injera Bread

This flat bread is probably the most popular one in Ethiopia. It's included in almost every meal. The best thing is that it's very easy to make! You'll see!

Preparation time: 3 days

Total time: 3 days and 10 minutes

Yield: 10

Ingredients:

- 2 cups water
- 1 and ½ cups teff finely grounded
- Salt to the taste
- Vegetable oil for frying

Method:

1. In a bowl, mix teff with water, cover with a towel and leave aside in a dark place for 3 days.

2. After time has passed, uncover bowl, add salt and stir well until you obtain a batter.

3. Heat up a pan over medium heat, grease it with some vegetable oil, pour ¼ cup of batter, spread evenly in a thin layer in the pan rotating it in the air, cook for almost 1 minute, flip and cook until it's done on the side.

4. Transfer to a plate and repeat the action with the rest of the injera batter.

5. Serve after they are cold enough.

Enjoy!

Delicious Ambasha Bread

It only takes a few minutes to make this delicious bread. Try it!

Preparation time: 60 minutes

Total time: 1 hour and 20 minutes

Yield: 4

Ingredients:

- 1 and 1/3 cup water
- 1 package yeast
- 2 cups white flour
- ½ teaspoon salt
- 1/3 cup extra virgin olive oil
- 2 and ½ teaspoons baking powder

Method:

1. In a bowl, mix yeast with water and stir very well.

2. Add oil, flour, salt and baking powder, knead very well for 5 minutes until you obtain a dough.

3. Cover bowl, leave aside for 1 hour and knead ball into a circle.

4. Heat up a pan over medium high heat, add dough, fry for 10 minutes, flip and fry for another 10 minutes until it becomes golden.

5. Serve right away!

Enjoy!

Ethiopian Honey Bread

It's another great idea you need to try!

Preparation time: 2 hours

Total time: 3 hours

Yield: 1 loaf

Ingredients:

- 1 egg
- ¼ ounce dry yeast
- ½ cup honey
- 1 cup warm milk
- 4 and ½ cups white flour
- ¼ cup warm water
- 1 tablespoon coriander
- 6 tablespoons butter already melted
- 1 teaspoon salt
- ¼ teaspoon ground cloves
- ½ teaspoon cinnamon

Method:

1. In a bowl, mix yeast with water, stir and leave aside for 3 minutes.

2. Stir again and leave bowl in a warm place for 5 minutes.

3. In another bowl, mix honey with egg, milk, cinnamon, coriander, salt and cloves and stir very well.

4. Add yeast mix and 4 tablespoons butter and stir extremely well again.

5. Add flour gradually and stir until you obtain a dough.

6. Transfer dough to a floured surface and knead it for a few minutes.

7. Rub your hands with butter, knead butter for 5 more minutes, shape a ball, transfer to a bowl, cover and leave in a warm place for 1 hour.

8. Spread the rest of the butter on a loaf pan, knead dough for 2 more minutes, arrange it in the pan and leave it aside in a warm place for 1 more hour.

9. Introduce bread in the oven at 300 degrees F and bake it for 1 hour.

10. Take bread out of the oven, leave it aside to cool down, cut and serve it with butter.

Enjoy!

Ethiopian Instant Bread (Kita Firfir)

It's going to be the star element of your dinner party!

Preparation time: 10 minutes

Total time: 30 minutes

Yield: 3

Ingredients:

- 1 and ½ cups whole wheat flour
- 3 tablespoons clarified butter
- ½ cup barley flour
- ¼ teaspoon cardamom
- 1 tablespoon berbere mix
- 1 teaspoon baking powder
- Salt and black pepper to the taste
- 2 cups water

Method:

1. In a bowl, mix wheat flour with barley flour and baking powder and stir well.

2. Add water gradually and knead until you obtain a smooth dough.

3. Transfer dough to a pancake pan, flatten it, make some holes with a fork, place on stove on low heat and cook until it's gold on both sides.

4. Remove bread from heat, cut in small pieces and leave aside.

5. Heat up a small pan over low heat, add butter, berbere, cardamom, salt and pepper to the taste.

6. Mix bread with butter and serve right away.

Enjoy!

Ethiopian Steamed Bread (Hibist)

This is definitely a kind of bread you've never tried until now!

Preparation time: 2 hours

Total time: 2 hours and 45 minutes

Yield: 1 big loaf

Ingredients:

- 4 and ½ cups wheat flour
- 2 teaspoons yeast
- 1 teaspoon salt
- 4 teaspoons sugar
- 1 cup oil
- 3 and ½ cups water
- Water for steaming

Method:

1. In a bowl, mix yeast with salt, sugar and water, stir well and leave aside for 5 minutes.

2. Add oil and flour and stir well until you obtain a dough.

3. Knead your dough for 10-15 minutes, shape a ball, transfer to a bowl, cover with a towel and keep in a warm place for 2 hours.

4. Transfer dough to a floured surface, knead again for 2-3 minutes, shape a ball and arrange in a round baking dish which you've greased with some oil and covered with high quality tin foil.

5. Put water in a pot, place on stove and heat up.

6. Place the baking dish with the dough on top and steam on medium high heat for 45 minutes.

7. Take off heat, allow it to cool down, uncover, transfer to a cutting board, cut and serve.

Enjoy!

Chapter 3. Special Ethiopian Salad Recipes

It's now time to be really surprised with some of the best Ethiopian salad recipes. Just pay attention!

Delicious Azifa (Green Lentils Salad)

This salad is very popular in Ethiopia! Try this one as an appetizer for your next dinner party and serve with Injera bread!

Preparation time: 10 minutes

Total time: 55 minutes

Yield: 4

Ingredients:

- 1 cup green lentils already soaked
- 1 red onion finely chopped
- 2 tomatoes chopped
- 1 green chili pepper chopped
- ½ teaspoon mustard
- Salt and black pepper to the taste
- 5 tablespoons extra virgin olive oil
- 4 tablespoons lemon juice

Method:

1. Put lentils in a pot, add water to cover, place on stove and bring to a boil over medium high heat.

2. Cook lentils for 50 minutes, drain water, transfer to a bowl and mash them well.

3. Add tomatoes, chili pepper, onion, salt, black pepper, lemon juice and olive oil and toss to coat.

4. Keep in the fridge until you serve with the best Injera bread at your dinner party.

Enjoy!

Special Ethiopian Tomato Salad

It's just great! You don't need to know anything else!

Preparation time: 10 minutes

Total time: 10 minutes

Yield: 4

Ingredients:

- 2 cups tomatoes roughly chopped
- ¼ cup sweet onion finely chopped
- 1 and ½ cups cucumbers chopped
- 1 green hot chili pepper diced
- 2 teaspoons red wine vinegar
- 4 teaspoons lemon juice
- Salt and black pepper to the taste
- 2 teaspoons extra virgin olive oil

Method:

1. Put tomatoes in a salad bowl.

2. Add onion and cucumber and stir gently.

3. Add chili pepper, salt and black pepper to the taste and lemon juice.

4. Add the oil, toss to coat and serve right away.

Enjoy!

Delicious Eggplant Salad

It's a great and hearty choice for dinner!

Preparation time: 5 minutes

Total time: 20 minutes

Yield: 10

Ingredients:

- 2 eggplants chopped
- 3 garlic cloves chopped
- ¼ cup extra virgin olive oil
- Salt and black pepper to the taste
- 2 teaspoons sugar
- 3 cups black eyed peas already cooked
- 3 tablespoons lemon juice

Method:

1. Heat up a pan with the oil over medium high heat, add eggplant pieces, stir and cook for 8 minutes.

2. Add garlic, stir and cook for 1 more minutes.

3. Add sugar, peas, lemon juice, salt and pepper to the taste, stir, reduce heat to medium and cook for 3-4 minutes.

4. Transfer to a bowl, allow it to cool down and serve.

Enjoy!

Ethiopian Potato Salad

It's a very easy salad you'll definitely enjoy!

Preparation time: 10 minutes

Total time: 30 minutes

Yield: 6

Ingredients:

- 1 pound potatoes peeled and cut in chunks
- Juice from 1 lemon
- 1/3 cup white onion finely chopped
- 3 tablespoons grape seed oil
- 2 tablespoons parsley finely chopped
- Salt and white pepper to the taste
- 1 jalapeno pepper chopped

Method:

1. Put potatoes in a pot, cover them with water, bring to a boil over medium high heat, cook for 20 minutes, drain, rinse and put in a salad bowl.

2. In a small bowl, mix the oil with parsley, jalapeno, salt, pepper and onion and stir very well.

3. Mix dressing with potatoes, toss to coat and serve right away.

Enjoy!

Amazing Ethiopian Green Salad

It's a healthy and colored salad!

Preparation time: 5 minutes

Total time: 5 minutes

Yield: 4

Ingredients:

- 1 tablespoon white wine vinegar
- 1 tablespoon extra-virgin olive oil
- Salt and black pepper to the taste
- ½ teaspoon ginger finely grated
- 1 small garlic clove chopped
- 1 jalapeno pepper finely chopped
- ½ green leaf lettuce roughly chopped
- 1 small yellow onion finely chopped
- 1 red bell pepper chopped

Method:

1. In a small bowl, mix vinegar with the oil, salt and pepper to the taste, garlic, ginger and the jalapeno and stir very well.

2. In a salad bowl mix lettuce with onion and bell pepper.

3. Add salad dressing, toss to coat and serve.

Enjoy!

Ethiopian Beet and Potato Salad

It's a special salad with such a special taste!

Preparation time: 10 minutes

Total time: 1 hour

Yield: 8

Ingredients:

- 15 ounces yellow potatoes roughly chopped
- 15 ounces red beet chopped
- 2 tablespoons peanut oil
- 1 small yellow onion chopped
- ¼ cup lemon juice
- 1 jalapeno chili chopped
- A pinch of fenugreek seeds
- Salt and black pepper to the taste
- ¼ teaspoon mustard seeds

Method:

1. Put beet in a pan, cover with water, place on stove over medium high heat, bring to a boil, cook for 45 minutes, drain water, put them in a bowl and leave aside.

2. Put potatoes in another pot at the same time as the beet pieces, cover with water, bring to a boil, cook for 25 minutes, drain and mix them with the beet.

3. In a small bowl mix onion with chili pepper, lemon juice and oil and stir very well.

4. Combine this with beet and potatoes, add salt and pepper and toss to coat.

5. Put mustard seeds in a pan, heat up over medium high heat and toast them for a few seconds.

6. Add them to the salad, also add fenugreek seeds, stir and serve right away.

Enjoy!

Chapter 4. Delicious Ethiopian Soups and Stews

You only deserve the best. Therefore here are the most delicious Ethiopian soups and stews. Prepare yourself!

Tomato and Lentil Soup (Shorba Addis)

It's a very rich soup which tastes so..so good!

Preparation time: 10 minutes

Total time: 55 minutes

Yield: 3

Ingredients:

- 1 carrot chopped
- 1 small yellow onion chopped
- 3 garlic cloves finely chopped
- 1 teaspoon ginger finely grated
- 1 tablespoon berbere
- ¼ cup tomato paste
- 2 and ½ cups veggie stock
- 1 teaspoon fenugreek seeds
- 1 potato chopped
- ¼ cup brown lentils
- ¼ cup orzo pasta (whole wheat)

Method:

1. Heat up a pot over medium high heat, add onion, stir and cook for 2-3 minutes.

2. Reduce heat to medium low, add berbere, carrot, garlic and ginger, stir and cook for 1 more minute.

3. Add fenugreek seeds, stir and cook for 2 minutes.

4. Add stock and tomato paste and bring to a boil.

5. Add lentils, stir, cover pot, reduce heat to low and simmer for 25 minutes.

6. Add orzo, stir, cover again and boil for 5 minutes.

7. Pour into soup bowls and serve right away.

Enjoy!

Special Ethiopian Carrot Soup

This is easy to make and it's one of the most popular Ethiopian soups.

Preparation time: 5 minutes

Total time: 35 minutes

Yield: 3

Ingredients:

- 7 carrots chopped
- 1 yellow onion chopped
- 2 potatoes, peeled and chopped
- 4 teaspoons coriander powder
- 1 teaspoon turmeric
- 1 teaspoon garlic finely chopped
- 2 inch piece ginger finely chopped
- A drizzle of vegetable oil
- ½ teaspoons mekelesha
- Salt and white pepper to the taste

Method:

1. Heat up a pot with a drizzle of vegetable oil over medium high heat, add onion and cook for 1 minute stirring all the time.

2. Add carrots and potatoes, stir and cook for 2 more minutes.

3. Add coriander, garlic, turmeric and ginger, stir and cook for 1 minute more.

4. Add water to cover veggies, reduce heat to medium and simmer for 25 minutes.

5. Blend your carrot soup well using your kitchen blender, add salt, white pepper and the mekelesha, stir well, pour into soup bowls and serve.

Enjoy!

Delicious Ethiopian Chicken and Butter Soup

It's going to make you try it over and over again! That's how good it is!

Preparation time: 5 minutes

Total time: 55 minutes

Yield: 6

Ingredients:

- 13 ounces already cooked butter beans
- 1 chicken cut into pieces
- 13 ounces carrots chopped
- 13 ounces potatoes chopped
- 13 ounces yellow onion chopped
- 1 spring rosemary
- 2 teaspoons turmeric
- 2 inches cube kibe (Ethiopian butter)
- 2 inches ginger finely chopped
- Salt to the taste
- 2 teaspoons vegetable oil

Method:

1. Heat up a pot with the oil over medium high heat, add chicken pieces and salt, stir and cook for 5 minutes.

2. Add ginger, onion and turmeric, stir again and cook for 6 more minutes.

3. Add potatoes and carrots and cook for 5 more minutes.

4. Add butter beans, Ethiopian butter and rosemary and stir again.

5. Add water to cover, bring to a boil, reduce heat to medium and simmer for 20 minutes.

6. Stir and cook for another 10 minutes.

7. Add salt, pour in bowls and serve.

Enjoy!

Delicious Ethiopian Beetroot Soup

If you are in the mood for a really authentic Ethiopian soup, then this is it!

Preparation time: 5 minutes

Total time: 35 minutes

Yield: 4

Ingredients:

- 4 beets roughly chopped
- 1 carrot chopped
- 2 potatoes chopped
- 1 yellow onion chopped
- 1 teaspoon garlic finely chopped
- Salt to the taste
- 2 teaspoons vegetable oil
- 1 teaspoon mitmita
- 2 teaspoons beso bela

Method:

1. Heat up a pot with the oil over medium high heat, add onions, mitmita and garlic, stir and cook for 4 minutes.

2. Add beets, potatoes and carrot, stir and cook for another 4 minutes.

3. Add beso bela, stir and cook for 2 minutes.

4. Add water to cover, bring to a boil, reduce heat to medium and simmer soup for 20 minutes.

5. Add salt to the taste, blend your soup well using your kitchen blender, pour into soups and serve right away.

Enjoy!

Amazing Ethiopian Chicken Stew

It's so delicious! You'll love it!

Preparation time: 10 minutes

Total time: 1 hour and 10 minutes

Yield: 6

Ingredients:

- 1 whole chicken cut in pieces
- 3 yellow onions chopped
- ¼ cup canola oil
- ½ tablespoon ginger finely grated
- ½ tablespoon paprika
- 1 tablespoon garlic finely minced
- 3 tablespoons spiced butter
- 1 tablespoon tomato paste
- 1 tablespoon basil finely chopped
- 6 eggs hard boiled and peeled
- 2 tablespoons berbere
- Salt and black pepper to the taste
- 3 cups water

Method:

1. Heat up a pot with the oil over medium high heat, add spiced butter and the onion, stir and cook for 8 minutes.

2. Add garlic, ginger and berbere, stir and cook for 5-6 more minutes.

3. Add chicken pieces, salt and pepper, paprika, tomato paste, basil and the water, bring to a boil, cover pot and cook your stew for 30 minutes.

4. Add the eggs, cook for 10 more minutes, transfer to plates and serve right away.

Enjoy!

The Best Ethiopian Stew (Alicha)

It's really simple to make and it will make you feel amazing! Try it!

Preparation time: 5 minutes

Total time: 35 minutes

Yield: 4

Ingredients:

- 6 potatoes chopped
- 5 carrots chopped
- 1 and ½ cups red onion finely chopped
- 1 and ½ cups vegetable oil
- ¼ teaspoon garlic finely chopped
- 1 cabbage chopped
- 6 chili peppers chopped
- Salt and black pepper to the taste
- 2 tablespoons parsley finely chopped
- 1 teaspoon cardamom
- 1 teaspoon nutmeg
- 2 tablespoons fresh basil finely chopped

Method:

1. Heat up a pot with the oil over medium high heat, add onion and cook for 4-5 minutes.

2. Add potatoes, carrots, cabbage, garlic, chili peppers, stir, cover, reduce heat to medium and cook for 30 minutes.

3. Add salt and pepper to the taste, cardamom, nutmeg, parsley and basil, stir and cook for 8 more minutes.

4. Transfer to plates and serve.

Enjoy!

Wonderful Ethiopian Pumpkin Stew

You don't need anything else! Just gather your friends and enjoy it!

Preparation time: 10 minutes

Total time: 1 hour

Yield: 6

Ingredients:

- 1 yellow onion finely chopped
- 2 tablespoons of vegetable oil
- 1 inch ginger piece finely chopped
- 1 pumpkin cut in medium wedges
- 2 teaspoons berbere
- 3 tablespoons tomato puree
- 2 cups water
- Salt to the taste
- ¼ cup parsley finely chopped

Method:

1. Heat up a pot with the oil over the medium heat, add onion, stir and cook for 5 minutes.

2. Add berbere and ginger, stir and cook for 1 minute.

3. Add pumpkin wedges, water, salt to the taste and the tomato puree, stir, bring to a boil and cook for 35 minutes.

4. Add chopped parsley at the end, stir gently, transfer to serving plates and serve.

Enjoy!

Tasty Ethiopian Beef Stew

It's just awesome! You'll see!

Preparation time: 30 minutes

Total time: 1 hour and 30 minutes

Yield: 6

Ingredients:

For the berbere:

- ¼ teaspoon nutmeg
- ½ teaspoon cumin
- 1 teaspoon fenugreek seeds
- ¼ teaspoon turmeric
- ½ teaspoon black pepper
- 4 tablespoons hot chili flakes
- 1 teaspoon dried ginger
- 2 tablespoons paprika
- 2 teaspoons dry onion flakes
- ¾ teaspoon cardamom
- ¼ teaspoon allspice
- ½ teaspoon garlic powder
- 1 teaspoon coriander powder
- ½ teaspoon ground cloves
- ½ teaspoon cinnamon

For the stew:

- 3 tablespoons vegetable oil
- 2 tablespoons Ethiopian butter
- 1 and ½ pounds beef meat cut in small cubes
- 2 garlic cloves finely chopped
- 1 yellow onion finely chopped
- 2 tablespoons tomato paste
- 2 teaspoons berbere
- ½ teaspoon sugar
- Salt and black pepper to the taste
- 2 cups beef broth

Method:

1. First you need to prepare the berbere mix.

2. In a pan, mix nutmeg, cumin, fenugreek.

3. Add turmeric, ½ teaspoon black pepper, chili flakes, ginger, paprika, onion flakes, cardamom, allspice, garlic powder, coriander powder, cloves and cinnamon.

4. Heat everything up over high heat, toast for a few minutes, stirring all the time, transfer to a coffee grinder and ground well.

5. Put berbere spice in a container, keep in a dark place and reserve 2 teaspoons for the beef stew.

6. Heat up a pot with the oil over medium high heat, add butter and the onion.

7. Stir well, cook for 3-4 minutes and mix with berbere, garlic, tomato paste and sugar.

8. Add some of the broth and stir until you obtain a paste.

9. Add meat, the rest of the broth, salt and pepper to the taste, cover pot and simmer over medium heat for about 1 hour.

10. Add more salt and pepper if needed, transfer to plates and serve.

Enjoy!

Ethiopian Lentils Stew

It's one of the healthiest stews you'll ever have!

Preparation time: 10 minutes

Total time: 45 minutes

Yield: 4

Ingredients:

- 1 cup lentils soaked overnight
- 1 yellow onion chopped
- 2 tablespoons coconut oil
- ¼ cup cooking oil
- 2 teaspoons garlic finely chopped
- 1 and ½ tablespoons berbere
- 2 teaspoons smoked paprika
- 1 teaspoon cumin
- ½ tablespoons ginger finely grated
- 2 cups veggie stock
- 1 tablespoon tomato paste
- 2 green onions finely chopped
- Salt and black pepper to the taste
- 2 tablespoons parsley finely chopped

Method:

1. Heat up a pan with the coconut and cooking oil over medium high heat, add yellow onion, stir and cook for 3-4 minutes.

2. Add garlic, berbere, paprika, cumin and ginger, stir and cook for 4 more minutes.

3. Add lentils, tomato paste, veggie stock and green onions, bring to a boil, reduce heat to medium, cover and cook for 30 minutes.

4. Add salt and pepper to the taste, sprinkle parsley, stir gently, transfer to plates and serve.

Enjoy!

Chapter 5. Authentic Ethiopian Main Courses

All you have to do is to pay attention and follow all the steps and you will have some of the most amazing Ethiopian main courses ready in no time! Enjoy them!

Delicious Ethiopian Steak

It's going to amaze you with its special taste and texture.

Preparation time: 1 hour

Total time: 1 hour and 45 minutes

Yield: 6

Ingredients:

- 1 and ½ tablespoons berbere spice
- 1 and ½ pounds sirloin steak
- 1 pint cherry tomatoes cut in halves
- 1 pint yellow cherry tomatoes cut in halves
- 2 tablespoons lemon juice
- Salt and black pepper to the taste
- 2 tablespoons olive oil
- 3 celery ribs thinly sliced
- 2 tablespoons capers already drained and chopped
- 2 tablespoons parsley finely chopped
- 4 tablespoons butter
- 1 small red onion thinly sliced
- 2 teaspoons red wine vinegar
- Lettuce leaves for serving

Method:

1. Mix steak with 1 tablespoon berbere, put in a bowl and leave aside for 1 hour.

2. Arrange all cherry tomatoes in a baking dish, drizzle olive oil on top, add salt and pepper, introduce in the oven at 350 degrees F and bake for 45 minutes.

3. In a bowl, mix the rest of the berbere with lemon juice, celery, vinegar, parsley, capers and onion and stir well.

4. Add salt and pepper to the taste and stir again.

5. Meanwhile, heat up a large pan with the butter over medium high heat, add steak, season with salt and pepper, and cook for 5 minutes on each side.

6. Transfer steak to a cutting board, leave aside for 10 minutes and slice.

7. Arrange steak on lettuce leaves and serve with celery and onion mix and with baked tomatoes on the side.

Enjoy!

Ethiopian Sautéed Fish Dish (Yasa Tibs)

It's great for dinner!

Preparation time: 1 hour

Total time: 1 hour and 7 minutes

Yield: 2

Ingredients:

- Juice from 4 limes
- 1 and ½ teaspoon berbere
- 2 cod fillets, boneless, cut in chunks
- 2 tablespoons extra virgin olive oil
- ¼ cup fish stock
- 1 teaspoon paprika
- ¼ cup tomato paste
- 2 inch piece ginger finely grated
- 2 tablespoons sesame oil
- 3 garlic cloves finely chopped
- 1 tablespoon coriander finely chopped

Method:

1. In a bowl, mix fish with lime juice and the berbere, cover and leave aside for 1 hour.

2. Heat up a pan with the sesame and olive oil over medium high heat.

3. Add paprika, garlic and ginger, stir and cook for 3-4 minutes.

4. Add fish with its liquids, tomato paste and fish stock, stir gently and cook for 3 more minutes.

5. Stir again and cook for 2 more minutes.

6. Take off heat, arrange on serving plates, sprinkle coriander on top and serve with injera bread.

Enjoy!

Amazing Ethiopian Chicken

It's one of the best chicken based main dishes ever!

Preparation time: 10 minutes

Total time: 1 hour

Yield: 4

Ingredients:

- 16 chicken wings
- 2/3 cup soy sauce
- 1 yellow onion chopped
- ½ teaspoon cinnamon
- ½ teaspoon cloves finely ground
- 1/8 teaspoon ginger finely ground

Method:

1. Put chicken wings in a pot, add onion, add water to cover, place on stove, bring to a boil over medium heat, cover pot and cook for 20 minutes.

2. Meanwhile, heat up a pan over medium heat, add soy sauce, cloves, cinnamon and gingers, stir and cook for 2-3 minutes.

3. Drain water from chicken wings, add to soy mix, stir gently and take off heat.

4. Transfer chicken wings and sauce to a baking dish, introduce in the oven at 375 degrees F and bake for 15 minutes.

5. Take out of the oven, arrange on a serving platter and serve.

Enjoy!

Amazing Ethiopian Spinach and Cottage Cheese

It's going to be the best party dish you'll ever have! Your guests will enjoy it for sure!

Preparation time: 10 minutes

Total time: 15 minutes

Yield: 4

Ingredients:

- 15 ounces cottage cheese
- 1/8 teaspoon ground cloves
- 1 garlic clove finely chopped
- 1 tablespoon fresh ginger finely grated
- 2 tablespoons soft butter
- ½ teaspoon cardamom
- 4 tablespoons yellow onion finely chopped
- 1 green chili pepper finely chopped
- 20 ounces spinach roughly chopped
- 2 garlic clove finely chopped

Method:

1. In a bowl, mix cheese with cloves, 1 garlic clove and cardamom, stir well, cover and keep in the fridge for now.

2. Heat up a pan with the butter over medium heat, add onion and cook for 1-2 minutes stirring all the time.

3. Add chili pepper, ginger and 2 garlic cloves, stir and cook for 5 more minutes.

4. Add spinach, cook for a few minutes and take off heat.

5. Drain excess liquid, transfer spinach to plates and top with cottage cheese mix.

6. Serve right away.

Enjoy!

Great Ethiopian Lamb

It's amazing, it's exotic and it's fabulous! It's the best Ethiopian lamb dish! You can serve it with injera bread!

Preparation time: 1 hour

Total time: 1 hour and 20 minutes

Yield: 4

Ingredients:

- 1 cup red wine
- 3.5 ounces butter
- 2 teaspoons saffron
- 1 teaspoon coriander
- 1 teaspoon sweet paprika
- 1 tablespoon brown sugar
- 2 pounds lamb meat
- 3 garlic cloves finely chopped
- 1 red onion finely chopped
- 2 red bell peppers chopped
- A pinch of ground nutmeg
- Salt and black pepper to the taste

Method:

1. In a bowl, mix lamb with onion, wine and bell peppers, cover and leave aside for 1 hour.

2. Heat up a pan with the butter over medium heat, add garlic cloves, saffron, nutmeg and coriander.

3. Stir, cook for 2 minutes and then add sugar paprika.

4. Stir, add lamb and cook until meat is done.

5. Season with salt and pepper to the taste, stir gently one more time, transfer to plates and serve right away.

Enjoy!

Ethiopian Beef Steak Tartar

It's also called Kitfo and we guarantee you will adore it!

Preparation time: 25 minutes

Total time: 40 minutes

Yield: 6

Ingredients:

- 2 pounds beef trimmed and cut into medium pieces
- 1 teaspoon cardamom powder
- 6 teaspoons cayenne pepper
- 4 tablespoons Ethiopian butter
- Salt and black pepper to the taste
- ¼ teaspoon garlic powder

Method:

1. In a food processor, mix half of the meat with half of the cayenne pepper and blend well.

2. Add more meat and cayenne pepper and blend well again.

3. Add the rest of the meat and the rest of the cayenne pepper and blend well again.

4. Heat up a pan with the butter over medium high heat, add cardamom, garlic powder, salt and pepper, stir well and take off heat.

5. Mix meat with butter and stir until it combines.

6. Arrange on a warm plate and serve right away.

Enjoy!

Chapter 6. The Most Popular Ethiopian Drinks Recipes

You will now be able to discover some of the most amazing Ethiopian drinks. They all are wonderful!

Ethiopian Spiced Tea

It's an infusion you'll love!

Preparation time: 2 minutes

Total time: 6 minutes

Yield: 2

Ingredients:

- 1/8 teaspoon ground cloves
- ½ teaspoon nutmeg
- 1 cup water
- 1 inch piece ginger sliced
- ½ teaspoon cinnamon
- 1 teaspoon ground cardamom

Method:

1. In a bowl, mix cloves with nutmeg, cinnamon and cardamom well.

2. Put water in a pot, bring to a boil, add 1/8 teaspoon mixed spice and the ginger and boil for 4 minutes.

3. Strain liquid in a cup and serve right away.

Enjoy!

Ethiopian Punch

On your next party, try something different! Let's forget about the regular punch and try a new one: an Ethiopian one!

Preparation time: 10 minutes

Total time: 10 minutes

Yield: 16

Ingredients:

- 1 cup maraschino cherry juice
- 1 cup raspberry syrup
- 1 cup lemon juice
- 1 cup orange juice
- 1 cup pineapple juice
- 2 and ½ quarts sparkling water
- 1 cup grape juice
- Orange slices for serving

Method:

1. In a large punch bowl, mix raspberry syrup with maraschino, orange and lemon juice.

2. Add pineapple and grape juice and stir.

3. Add sparkling water and orange slices at the end.

4. Serve right away!

Enjoy!

Ethiopian Telba

It's healthy and it's very refreshing. Try it sometimes!

Preparation time: 10 minutes

Total time: 20 minutes

Yield: 6

Ingredients:

- 6 cups hot water
- 2 tablespoons honey
- 1 cup flax seed

Method:

1. Heat up a pan over low heat, add flaxseed, roast for 10 minutes stirring all the time, take off heat and leave aside to completely cool down.

2. Transfer flaxseed into a coffee grinder and grind until you obtain a powder.

3. Transfer powder to a bowl, add hot water, stir, cover and leave aside for 10 minutes.

4. Strain into a glass, add honey, stir well and serve when it's cold.

Enjoy!

Tej (Ethiopian Honey Wine)

It's a special Ethiopian drink you can serve on a special occasion.

Preparation time: 10 minutes

Total time: 10 minutes

Yield: 6

Ingredients:

- 2 cups white wine
- 1 cup honey
- 2 cups water

Method:

1. In a pitcher, mix wine with honey and stir extremely well.

2. Add water, stir again, introduce in the fridge and serve after it's really cold.

Enjoy!

Delicious Ethiopian Coffee (Kahawa)

There's nothing like a good cup of coffee!

Preparation time: 5 minutes

Total time: 20 minutes

Yield: 4

Ingredients:

- 4 tablespoons ground coffee
- 2 cardamom pods
- 4 cups water
- 1 teaspoon grated ginger

Method:

1. Put water in a pot, heat up over medium high heat, add cardamom, bring to a boil and simmer for 10 minutes.

2. Reduce heat after 10 minutes, add coffee and ginger and simmer for another 5 minutes.

3. Turn off heat, strain coffee, add sweetener if needed and serve.

Enjoy!

Conclusion

It's a fact! Ethiopian cuisine is fascinating. We are totally sure you've never thought that Ethiopian food could taste so good! We know you've never imagined Ethiopian dishes to be so full of rich flavors, textures and smells.

We've given you the chance to find out everything about Ethiopian foods.

We've brought into your homes the most delicious, popular and unique Ethiopian dishes.

Try each and enjoy some of the most fabulous meals ever!

About the Author

Martha is a chef and a cookbook author. She has had a love of all things culinary since she was old enough to help in the kitchen, and hasn't wanted to leave the kitchen since. She was born and raised in Illinois, and grew up on a farm, where she acquired her love for fresh, delicious foods. She learned many of her culinary abilities from her mother; most importantly, the need to cook with fresh, homegrown ingredients if at all possible, and how to create an amazing recipe that everyone wants. This gave her the perfect way to share her skill with the world; writing cookbooks to spread the message that fresh, healthy food really can, and does, taste delicious. Now that she is a mother, it is more important than ever to make sure that healthy food is available to the next generation. She hopes to become a household name in cookbooks for her delicious recipes, and healthy outlook.

Martha is now living in California with her high school sweetheart, and now husband, John, as well as their infant daughter Isabel, and two dogs; Daisy and Sandy. She is a stay at home mom, who is very much looking forward to expanding their family in the next few years to give their daughter some siblings. She enjoys cooking with, and for, her family and friends, and is waiting impatiently for the day she can start cooking with her daughter.

For a complete list of my published books, please, visit my Author's Page...

https://www.amazon.com/author/martha-stephenson

Author's Afterthoughts

Thanks ever so much to each of my cherished readers for investing the time to read this book!

I know you could have picked from many other books but you chose this one. So a big thanks for downloading this book and reading all the way to the end.

If you enjoyed this book or received value from it, I'd like to ask you for a favor. Please take a few minutes to post an honest and heartfelt review on Amazon.com. Your support does make a difference and helps to benefit other people.

Thanks!

Martha Stephenson

CPSIA information can be obtained
at www.ICGtesting.com
Printed in the USA
LVOW11s1243090417
530173LV00003B/290/P